THE SOMEDAY SYNDROME

by
Rod Parsley

Christian Publishing Services, Inc.
Tulsa, Oklahoma

Unless otherwise indicated, all Scripture quotations are taken
from the *King James Version* of the Bible.

The Someday Syndrome
ISBN 0-88144-069-8
Copyright © 1986 by Rod Parsley
Word of Life Church
Columbus, Ohio

Published by Christian Publishing Services, Inc.
P. O. Box 55388
Tulsa, Oklahoma 74155

CONTENTS

ABOUT THE AUTHOR

Pastor Rod Parsley has been termed, by Dr. Lester Sumrall, as "one of the new breed." At age 29, he pastors a church with more than 3,000 members in Columbus, Ohio. As rapid growth continues, Pastor Parsley is leading his congregation into the ministry's fifth phase of building with construction under way for a 5,000-seat sanctuary.

As pastor of Word of Life Church, he is directly involved with the ministry's outreach programs, including a daily television and worldwide shortwave radio broadcast entitled *Breakthrough*. Pastor Parsley also travels extensively throughout the United States ministering with such men as Dr. Lester Sumrall and Norvel Hayes, as well as appearing on the Trinity Broadcasting Network and the PTL Network's Jim Bakker Show. His ability to present the Word of God, in dynamic fashion, produces a "Breakthrough" in the lives of many.

DEDICATION

This book is lovingly and respectfully dedicated to my uncle, the Rev. Edward D. Endicott, who had the courage to believe in me and gave me the courage to believe in myself.

INTRODUCTION

Throughout the years, religious tradition and lack of knowledge have perpetuated a prevailing attitude in the church world. This web of deception is otherwise known as the "Someday Syndrome." For those entangled in this web, a state of hopeless search has become the consequence of teaching that encourages them to look for a better tomorrow, for "someday."

A life of present-day victory has eluded many as they view Heaven as the only answer or pathway to joy, health, and freedom. In this book, we will examine how Jesus procured the very essence of Heaven and made it available to us on earth. Knowledge of such will facilitate our in-depth study and show you how to activate and release your faith in order to live the *zoe* — the God kind of life — and have Heaven on earth today!

1
THE SOMEDAY SYNDROME

The present-day Church is caught in, what I call, "the someday syndrome." This syndrome creates a cruel place that is darker than the Twilight Zone, for it compels men and women to live in everyday drudgery with nothing more to go on than a "search-for-tomorrow" hope.

The world, on every hand and on every street corner, is looking across the horizon for a better day. This "somewhere over the rainbow" concept, that has invaded our society, is understandable when you look at it from a natural standpoint. When social unrest runs rampant, when races are filled with such contempt for one another, and when corruption abounds in governments, it is not difficult to desire a better, or look for, a better tomorrow.

Looking back through the pages of history, it becomes apparent that there has never been permanent stability in nations or governments — which shows us that it has *never* gotten better since Adam bowed his knee to Satan in the Garden of Eden. The "good old days of yesteryear" are a myth because it has never been any better than it is right now in the world, and what is more, it is never going to be any better because *there is no stability in mankind outside of Jesus Christ.*

The sad thing, however, is that the Church has fallen into the same syndrome. Christian songs, church people, and even preachers constantly say, "Some day . . . when we all get to Heaven . . . life will get better." We hear, "Someday, someday, someday, we'll inhabit the place where God is." But the Spirit of God is here, and now, because the Bible says that Heaven is where Jesus is. Jesus is *in* us as well as *among* us on earth; therefore, Heaven is *in* us and *among* us.

Heaven is ours today if we simply partake of what is rightfully ours as heirs of the Promise. We don't want the death of Jesus on Calvary to be in vain in our lives, so we should want and receive all that was purchased on our behalf. When He climbed up Golgotha's hillside with the hot, Palestinian sun pitilessly beating down upon His open wounds until, I am sure, He felt as if the very flames of hell had imbedded themselves in His flesh. When He died of His own will on the cross, He did it to give great things to those who should be receiving them with great joy and gladness in their earthly lives.

The deeper truths and revelations of the Word, and of all that Jesus' sacrifice meant, are becoming more and more available to the Church. When great men of faith such as Kenneth Hagin and Kenneth Copeland first began teaching the messages of faith, healing, and prosperity across America, they were scorned by the majority of Christians. Now, however, instead of a few people attending their services in small buildings, it is hard to get within three country blocks of their meetings held in very large buildings, because people are beginning to recognize God's truth in what they have been saying.

The Church does not have to "understand it better by and by" because we have the knowledge and revelation now in the Word of God, if we will just receive it. Psalms 119:105 says, **Thy Word is a lamp unto my feet, and a light unto my path.**

The world scene may be horrible now, but it is not going to get any better — although it may look better from time to time — because the devil is not ignorant to what is going on. He sets the climate in society that breeds the "search-for-tomorrow" attitude where everything seemingly will get better. It is the attitude that everything in the past *was* better, but today is nowhere and nothing.

The devil is carefully establishing a climate where people search continually and ever more desperately for a better tomorrow. This search will springboard the Antichrist right into the middle of destruction and despair professing to have all the answers to the world's problems.

This Antichrist, or false Christ, will restore peace to the world for a certain period of time during which multiplied millions will flock to him and be pitifully deceived. They will believe that they will not have to live in poverty or sickness because he can provide an answer. They will believe that they do not have to live in wars and racial violence because he can establish peace. This picture of deception is not pretty and we, like Jeremiah, are to warn the people of what Satan is doing.

The frightening point is that even many Christians have allowed their lives to become such a hell on earth that the reign of the Antichrist will seem as if he just took them to Heaven! Seekers of the spectacular will flock to him because he'll have the power of the underworld regions at his command. He'll raise the dead, restore sight to the blind, speech to the dumb, hearing to the deaf, and provide an answer to every problem.

The blessed thing is that Jesus already has prepared an immunity vaccine against the Antichrist and his answers, and this vaccine is that *tomorrow already has come*. The future is here, and Jesus brought tomorrow to us today. The Bible tells us this in Luke, who wrote of a day when Jesus read to his neighbors, in his hometown, from the book of Isaiah.

> **And he came to Nazareth, where He had been brought up: and, as His custom was, he went into the synagogue on the sabbath day, and stood up for to read.**
>
> **And there was delivered unto Him the book of the prophet Esaias. And when he had opened the book, he found the place where it was written,**
>
> **The Spirit of the Lord is upon me, because he hath anointed me to preach the gospel to the poor; he hath sent me to heal the brokenhearted, to preach deliverance to the captives, and recovering of sight to the blind, to set at liberty them that are bruised.**
>
> **To preach the acceptable year of the Lord.**
>
> **Luke 4:16-19**

The "acceptable year of the Lord" was the Year of Jubilee. In Leviticus, chapter 25, we find that a Jubilee year was the last year in a 50-year period. For the first 49 years, the Israelites were allowed to take slaves, sow the fields, prune the vineyards, and gather the harvest, except that each seventh year was to be a sabbath for the land. Then at the beginning of the 50th year, after the seventh sabbath year in a row, the trumpet was to sound proclaiming a Jubilee. During this year, the ground was not to be worked, all slaves, who were Israelites, were to be set free, and all debts were erased. This year was to be a sabbath of rest unto the land and unto the Lord. During the 48th year, the Lord promised them a great three-year's-crop-in-one. This crop would sustain them over the seventh sabbath year (49th), the

Jubilee (50th), and until the first year's harvest of the new cycle.

If someone in Israel had run up the equivalent of a $40 million debt, that debt was to be erased as quickly as a $40 one. If one of their brother Israelites had been taken as a slave, he was to be set free from all bondage. The Lord God didn't even want the ground to be worked. He wanted it to rest as well during that 50th year, in spite of its having lain fallow the year before.

So when Jesus quoted Isaiah about the acceptable year of the Lord, He was proclaiming Jubilee. He was saying, in essence, that all slaves of Satan's bondage are set free. **If the Son therefore shall make you free, ye shall be free indeed** (John 8:36). When Jesus stood in the synagogue that day and opened up His blessed mouth and spoke the words, the trumpet sounded and will never have to sound again. *We are free.* The blood cries from Calvary that you are free. The Holy Spirit cries, "You're free. You're free." Glory to God!

I can imagine what it must have been like, in the Year of Jubilee, for a man who had been a slave for many long years, had not seen his family, and had to work hard tilling the ground. Perhaps he had felt the whip across his back, and lived in cramped slave quarters, when, suddenly, he began to hear the Trumpet of Jubilee blowing, even faintly in the distance.

Once I was in bondage to sin, wrapped up in sickness, disease, infirmity, and weakness. In the dark slave quarters of sin's dungeon, I began to hear a cry coming from the hillside of Golgotha. Jesus said, "You're free!" I don't believe that slave had to ask anyone for permission to leave. I believe he just looked for an open door; and, so can we. Jesus proclaimed our freedom on Calvary and, through this, opened the door for us.

You might ask, "What did he free us from?" In Luke 4:18, Jesus was proclaiming, "You are free from poverty, blindness, brokenheartedness, Satan's bondage, and being bruised." There continues to be a problem, however, the same problem Jesus' hearers had that day. Verse 21 says, **And he began to say to them,** ***This day*** **is this scripture fulfilled in your ears.**

He meant today, not tomorrow or the next day. *Today,* not tomorrow, *is the Year of Jubilee whereby we are free.* The scripture was fulfilled in their ears when Jesus spoke it out of His mouth. The words hit their eardrums, and they heard them. As we read on in Luke 4, we can see their reaction. They took Jesus out and tried to throw Him over a cliff.

Matthew says, in relating the same incident, **And he did not many mighty works there because of their unbelief** (Matt. 13:58). Later, however, Jesus went on to Capernaum where He preached the very same message and miracles abounded. The difference was that the people in Capernaum received the message, and the people in Nazareth did not. The thing that has always made the difference between those who live under the bondage of the curse of the law and those who live victorious and joyous lives is whether they hear the cry of the Year of Jubilee.

If you believe you will "get" it someday, that's exactly when you'll get it — someday, which is never. If you cannot believe you have freedom now, you will never believe you have it. If you believe that you have it *now,* you have it and that's all there is to it. *Faith is the title deed and the Word is the intangible substance that brings the spirit world into tangible reality in your life.* Faith will put your bills in order, your body in order, your mind in order, and your spirit in order with God. However, faith is only activated when you believe *now*.

On Calvary, Jesus looked over at one of the thieves hanging beside Him and said, **To day, shalt thou be with me in paradise** (Luke 23:43). Today, not tomorrow, is the Year of Jubilee whereby we *are* free. We should be ready, willing, and wanting to receive, not reject, what Jesus paid the price to purchase for us. That is why the "someday syndrome" is stealing victory from the Church. Satan knows that tomorrow never comes with God. God deals with the present because the past is over and tomorrow will never be here.

Hebrews 11:1 says, **Now faith is the substance of things hoped for, the evidence of things not seen.** When is faith the substance and the evidence? *Now*, right this moment. The devil knows this and that is why he tries to get Christians to think and to say, "When we get to Heaven, we'll be prosperous, free from sin, and free from sickness."

When we get to Heaven, when we get to Heaven, when we get to Heaven: by this attitude, Satan has robbed the blessing of the Year of Jubilee from many Christians, and made the death of Jesus of no effect in all but one area of their lives — their spirits. Jesus died on Calvary for more than just to get us to Heaven!

When Jesus said in Luke 9:1 that power and authority over devils was given to His disciples for their day, He was giving that same power and authority to us, as well, for our day. The devil is blinding us by getting our eyes on tomorrow. "How beautiful Heaven must be," people say. What is the matter with here?

"Well, Brother Parsley," some say, "it's so discouraging with sickness on every hand, troubles and trials, and woe is me, woe is me!"

The person who says that has been blinded by the lie of the Antichrist, the lie that gives the false hope that things will be better "tomorrow." Jesus stood up under the anointing and proclaimed the Year of Jubilee. Because of this, we are free today. When we became born again, we received the eternal life of God. Eternity has no beginning and no ending, and even death has no hold on the born-again believer.

Hebrews 9:27 says, **And as it is appointed unto men once to die, but after this the judgment.** If the life of eternity is in God, and God is in you, that means you are in eternity right now. You don't "go" to eternity when you die. In fact, if you have "died out" to the world, you will never *really* die again, for Jesus said, "If you live and believe in me, you will never die." (John 11:26.)

The Apostle Paul said, **O death, where is thy sting? O grave, where is thy victory?** (1 Cor. 15:55). There is no death to a born-again believer as he has already died the only death required of him. Paul also said, **I am crucified with Christ: nevertheless I live; yet not I, but Christ liveth in me . . .** (Gal. 2:20).

Did Jesus, after dying on the cross at Calvary, ever die again? Will He ever die again? When Paul died to the world, he did all the dying he was required by the Word of God to do. When he "died" on the Damascus road, he died. Paul said, **. . . Yet not I, but Christ liveth in me.** Christ is not death or dying and has nothing to do with anything that looks or talks like death, for God is the author of *life*! L-I-F-E, Life!

I can imagine the Apostle Paul as he sat in the Roman jail, and Nero sent down the letter informing him of his scheduled beheading. I can see Paul, as he rubs his fingernails on his garment, simply saying:

"You're going to kill me? I have already died my death on the Damascus Road. I'm not going to die. I am just going to be transformed." Hallelujah!

The only difference that physical death makes to the born-again believer is the transfer of the *zoe*-life of God, now living on Planet Earth, to Heaven. We don't have to wait until, all of a sudden, we get to Heaven to become healthy, free, wealthy, and wise. A victorious life is available on earth if we simply partake of it.

Jesus stood up in the midst of the synagogue at Nazareth and said, **This day is this scripture fulfilled in your ears.** If they had received His Word with gladness and put it to work in their lives, it would have worked. Jesus didn't die twice and neither did Paul. In fact, Revelation 7:14 says, These **have washed their robes, and made them white in the blood of the Lamb.** Revelation 20:6 says, **On such the second death has no power.** No *power!*

I had an uncle who gave his physical life on the battlefields of Vietnam in 1969. Listen, folks, he didn't feel one shot or feel the first pain because he was a man who pleased God. He was transformed into a new man. When we are born again, we receive the eternal life of God. This eternity has no beginning or ending, so, we merely step into the flow of it when we leave this world.

Jesus told the woman at the well, **Whosoever drinketh of the water that I shall give him shall never thirst** (John 4:14a). In John 7:38, Jesus said, **He that believeth on me, as the scripture hath said, out of his belly shall flow rivers of living water.** We must not let the devil blind us by getting our eyes on tomorrow because we are already free.

Make this confession and profession of your faith:

I am free!
I am alive, never to die!
Satan, I will not allow you to steal from me any longer. I am no longer in bondage, for Jesus has proclaimed unto me the Year of Jubilee, and I am free!

2
THE WORD OF LIFE

As we have learned in the previous chapter, Satan is attempting to blind the Church with the "someday syndrome." We know that people, buying this lie and running around looking for a better tomorrow, do not realize that this kind of climate and attitude will springboard the Antichrist into the world scene.

He will come at a time of world unrest and appear to have all of the answers to life's problems. We do not think the Church could be deceived, but how would a person feel if his baby was dying of cancer and this man had the cure? How would people feel if their sons and daughters were being slaughtered on the battlefields of war, in the Middle East, and this man came on the scene and said, "I'll proclaim peace in the world." Would there be those Christians who would listen?

There will be a lot of people, unaware of who he is, who will love the Antichrist because he has their needed answers. Do you realize whose fault this is? People will flock to the Antichrist by the multimillions, be deceived, and spend eternity with the devil in hell because we, the Church, have failed to give them answers to their problems.

In churches across the continents, there are people who need the power of God for healing; yet, they resist it. What are they looking for? Do they want to stay sick from now on? Do they want to be weak continually? No. But the devil has lied to them by saying, "Tomorrow you are going to get better." When we look for "tomorrow," we are caught in Satan's lie called the "someday syndrome."

The Antichrist's answers will appeal to those who have not been inoculated with the only vaccine to keep him from being attractive — the Word of God. John 17:17 says, **Sanctify them through thy truth:** *thy Word is truth.* And Proverbs 4:20-22 says:

> **My son, attend to my words; incline thine ear unto my sayings.**
>
> **Let them not depart from thine eyes; keep them in the midst of thine heart,**
>
> **For they are life unto those that find them, and health to all their flesh.**

The word *life*, used here, means "all things," not just physical existence. This specific word in the Greek is *zoe* and characterizes a spiritual life, a prosperous life, and a healthy and happy life. *Zoe* life is the life of our Creator and describes a God-kind of living found in the Word. When we discover and walk in the Word of God and in the truth thereof, then we naturally possess the life that the Word gives us, because God and the Word are one.

Notice that Proverbs 4:20 says, **My son, attend unto my** *words.* It doesn't say "attend to the Church or your grandmother or what Mom and Dad believe," but attend — or give attention to — *my words.* We find God's words in the Bible.

Then the writer goes on to tell why the son should attend to his words: **for they are** *life.* That verse says that they *are* life, not that they are going to be or hope to be or may be in Heaven, but that they *are* life right now. The phrase, "They are life," is cast in the present tense meaning *right now.*

22

The Word of God is life to you today, not tomorrow. The Word is health and healing to the body today, not tomorrow. The Word is not prosperity simply when we are walking the streets of gold in Heaven, but prosperity *today*. The Word is imparting life to us right now!

In John 11, we are told the story of Lazarus, the brother of Mary and Martha and the close friend of Jesus. One day, Martha walked up to Jesus and said, "Oh, Jesus, if you had only been here yesterday, my brother would not have died." She was looking at yesterday. Jesus then wept because of the sisters' unbelief, because He knew Lazarus would not remain in the tomb.

After which, Jesus went over to the tomb where his friend had lain for four days, as the Bible describes, **And when he thus had spoken, he cried out with a loud voice, Lazarus, come forth** (v.43). What made Lazarus come forth? The Word of God did, because the Word is the life-giving force in the world and there is no life outside God and His Word. That is why unsaved people are always searching, because they are lost and want to know what life is all about.

When Jesus comes on the scene, He speaks *words* of life; therefore, life exists. Those words don't float around the clouds, off in "tomorrow" somewhere. *The Words of Jesus are alive now!* The Word of God is the power of God, and that power is in the spoken Word. For example, in Isaiah 53:5, He tells us that we *are* healed and, if we speak that forth and believe it, we will release that power of life and, thus, receive healing.

When God speaks, worlds have no choice but to leap into existence. He stood out on nothing and said, **Let there be light: and there was light** (Gen. 1:30).

There was no question about it, because the Word went forth, therefore light was produced. Everything that God created, He spoke out of His blessed mouth, which is the creative force to bring forth physical manifestation in the earth.

When Jesus came face to face with the Gadarene demoniac and spoke the Word, the legion of unclean spirits had no choice but to obey the Word and leave. Glory to God for the power of His spoken Word whereby worlds exist, sickness dies, poverty vanishes, and life is begun! When Jesus comes into the face of death, it has no choice but to yield itself to life because *the Word is life.*

Acts 2:22-24 reveals to us that it was impossible for death to hold Jesus. That is an example of how strong His words are.

> **Ye men of Israel, hear these words; Jesus of Nazareth, a man approved of God among you by miracles and wonders and signs, which God did by him in the midst of you, as ye yourselves also know:**
>
> **Him, being delivered by the determinate counsel and foreknowledge of God, ye have taken, and by wicked hands have crucified and slain:**
>
> **Whom God hath raised up, having loosed the pains of death: because it was not possible that He should be holden of it.**

Jesus wasn't resurrected solely because He was the Son of God, but because the Word said He would be. David spoke concerning the resurrection of Jesus in one of his Psalms.

> **I have set the Lord always before me: because He is at my right hand, I shall not be moved.**
>
> **Therefore my heart is glad, and my glory rejoiceth: my flesh also shall rest in hope.**

For thou wilt not leave my soul in hell; neither wilt thou suffer thine Holy One to see corruption.

Thou wilt shew me the path of life: in thy presence is fulness of joy; at thy right hand there are pleasures forevermore.

Psalm 16:8-11

The Bible says that all scripture is inspired by the Holy Spirit, meaning it comes from the mouth of God. What raised Jesus from the tomb was the resurrecting power of the Word, because God inspired David to write the Psalms. The moment the Holy Spirit spoke to David while he was writing, God became eternally obligated, to Himself, to perform His Word.

God said He was not a man that He should lie. (Num. 23:19.) The Bible is His Word, not words of David or Paul or Luke. When Jesus was raised from the dead, God was simply performing the Word that He had already spoken. If *you* can find something in the Bible that will apply in the will of God for your life, it can be performed *in* your life, because God is eternally obligated to Himself to perform every minute detail of His Word.

God said that the world might pass away or burn up with fire but that His Word will stand. (Luke 21:33.) He is not speaking of the book called the Bible, necessarily, but the life-giving words which it contains. The Word is to be living on the inside of our beings. What Word is engrafted in our hearts is what God works with in our lives. If we believe and speak His Word forth, releasing our faith, God will perform it! Hallelujah!

If the disciples had understood what Psalm 16 really contained, they would not have gathered together in the upper room and mourned the death of Jesus.

If they had understood what the Word meant, they could have rejoiced and danced at Calvary because they would have known that God would perform His Word, thereby resurrecting Jesus. They would have realized that it was impossible for death to hold Jesus, yet they mourned and wept, just as we do, because we don't know the Word.

Hosea 4:6 says, **My people are destroyed for lack of knowledge.** We are not destroyed because the church is weak or the singers didn't sing pretty on Sunday, but through a lack of knowledge of God's Word. Let's go back to Acts 2:28 where Luke is quoting from the Old Testament:

> **Thou hast made known to me the ways of life; thou shalt make me full of joy with thy countenance.**

Notice that the ways of life, not death, are made known to us. In the second clause, Luke speaks of God's *countenance.* The word translated countenance means *in Thy Presence now and forever.* We shall be made full of joy in the presence of God now and forever, not just "someday" when we get to Heaven, but now!

Luke is quoting David's Psalm 16 with the exception of one word in the 11th verse, **Thou *wilt* show me the path of life.** In other words, he is saying, "You aren't *going* to show me someday. You've already shown me." In Psalms, David *was looking forward* to being shown the path of life. In Acts, they had *already found* the path of life. What is between the time of David and Luke that made that change?

The path of life was shown when Jesus died and rose again! When we die to this world, we die the only death required of us by the Word of God in Hebrews 9:27:

> **And as it is appointed unto men once to die, but after this the judgment.**

In John 11:25, Jesus said to Martha, **I am the resurrection, and the life.** He was saying, "I am, *right now,* the resurrection; and, I am, *right now,* the life." Then in the rest of verse 25 and in verse 26, He continued:

> He that believeth in me, though he were dead, yet shall he live,
> And whosoever liveth and believeth in me shall never die. Believest thou this?

Breaking down each phrase of this verse gives us a better understanding of the truth it contains.

1. **He that believeth in me:** If we are saved, then we believe that Jesus is the Son of God.

2. **Though he were dead:** Ephesians 2:1 tells us that we were dead in our trespasses and sins.

3. **Yet shall he live:** We don't have to believe, when we get to Heaven, because the believing part is already over because we are already there. Some people say, "We'll have victory over the devil in Heaven." However, the devil isn't going to be there! Why do you need victory over the devil in Heaven?

Now is when we need victory over the devil. *Now* is when we need victory over disease. *Now* is when we need victory over social unrest. Victory is not going to come "when we get to Heaven." Jesus intends for us to be victorious *right now* while we're in this world. The Bible says believing is faith, and faith wins the fight. So fight the good fight of faith!

4. **And whosoever liveth and believeth in me shall never die:** Once again, Jesus is telling us that if we have died to sin, we have died the only death required of us by the Word of God. The spirit part of us is alive and permeates every part of our existence forevermore.

In the last part of verse 26, Jesus asked Martha, **Believest thou this?** In other words, He is asking her,

"Do you believe, Martha, that if your brother believes in Me, he shall never die?" Martha then went from thinking about yesterday to thinking about tomorrow! She was under the impression that Jesus was speaking of the resurrection at the Last Day, but He was saying, "I am the resurrection and the life *today, right now.* If he believes and lives in Me, he shall never die."

The Church world has a group of present-day Marthas looking over the horizon to "someday." They say, "Oh, someday, I'll be well, when I get to Heaven." What difference does dying make? Dying is not the pathway to life. The Word is the the pathway to life.

God didn't say in Proverbs 4:20, "My son, attend unto death, for in it you will find health, happiness, and life." Yet, that is the way many people believe. It is as though they believe that death is some sort of cosmic force that suddenly transports us from a life of the natural to a spiritual life. If they do not have spiritual life now and are hoping to get it when they get to Heaven, forget it, because then it will be too late. We have to receive the life of God *now* because we get born again of the Spirit *now.*

The Bible teaches us that we should not be ignorant concerning Satan's devices. However, one of his principal tools against Christians is to get their minds off today and get them looking for a better tomorrow. God deals in the *now,* in *today.* This is a vital truth that the Church needs to learn.

Believe God *today,* not *tomorrow,* because *now* faith *is!* Release your faith and believe that God has met your needs today, *right now,* in accordance with His Word that seals it done!

3

ETERNAL LIFE —
A NEW DOORWAY

Let's look once again at Proverbs 4:20-22. The truth in this verse must be deposited into our spirits after which it can and will work for us. We need to put God's Word to work in our lives by activating it from our spirits, speaking it forth, and believing that it will transpire.

My son, attend to my words; incline thine ear unto my sayings.

Let them not depart from thine eyes; keep them in the midst of thine heart.

For they are life unto those that find them, and health to all their flesh.

The word *life*, used in verse 22, is defined for us in Ephesians 2:8:

For by grace are ye saved through faith; and that not of yourselves: it is the gift of God.

The word *saved*, in Greek, is translated *sozo*, meaning delivered, protected from, healed, rescued, done well to, and made whole. We have received all of those things by grace, which is the unmerited favor of God, and through faith, which is the activating medium. The life spoken of in Proverbs 4:20 agrees with *sozo*: both mean a life 100 percent free from poverty, sickness, sin, and the multitude of life's problems.

Once again, we receive this free life through grace and through faith. So let's explore the matter of faith as it appears in Hebrews, chapter 11. This chapter epitomizes faith by listing the heroes of faith who knew the "faith message" long before the Charismatic movement of today. They understood what walking in blind faith meant and were pleasing to God because of the greatness of it. Look specifically at the patriarch Noah in verse 7:

> **By faith Noah, being warned of God of things not seen as yet, moved with fear, prepared an ark to the saving of his house; by the which he condemned the world, and became heir of the righteousness which is by faith.**

The Bible is saying that, by faith, Noah prepared an ark to the saving of his household. All Noah had was the same ability as you and I, that of calling **those things which be not as though they were** (Rom. 4:17). It had never rained on the earth before; yet Noah, being moved by faith, ignored natural circumstances and built the ark. Years passed and it didn't rain, yet Noah knew, through the eyes of faith, that rain was coming!

Moses also was a man moved by faith regardless of the natural circumstances surrounding him. Through fear he left the king's house where he had been raised and went to the wilderness after he killed an Egyptian overseer who had been abusing one of the Hebrews — Moses' own race. But 40 years later, God appeared to him in a burning bush and instructed him to go back and lead his countrymen out of captivity.

Through faith Moses went, and through faith, he committed many marvelous exploits such as the Red Sea parting when he stretched out his rod. He was moved by faith, and the more he exercised his faith, the greater it grew.

Another hero of the Old Testament, Samson, went up against a lion by only one means: the realm of faith.

Hebrews 11 tells us of yet another hero called the "father of faith," a man named Abraham. He left his home and friends to sojourn in a place which God said he **should after receive for an inheritance** (v.8), yet Abraham went not knowing where it would be found. Hebrews 11:39 says:

> **And these all, having obtained a good report through faith, received not the promise.**

In the Greek, the verse is translated the same except for three words. It reads *fulfillment of the promise* instead of just *promise.*

> **And these all, having obtained a good report through faith, received not the fulfillment of the promise.**

This group of heroes received not the full promise but only part of it. These men certainly pleased God because of their great faith, yet they didn't receive the full promise. To explain this further, let's look at Hebrews 11:9,10.

> **By faith he sojourned in the land of promise, as in a strange country, dwelling in tabernacles with Isaac and Jacob, the heirs with him of the same promise:**
>
> **For he looked for a city which hath foundations, whose builder and maker is God.**

Abraham was in constant quest of a city whose builder and maker was God. The problem was that the actual place had not been revealed to him. One day, Abraham found that place, after the eyes that had seen much of God's promise fulfilled, finally closed in death. At that moment, he was ushered into the presence of God, and there Abraham found the city.

All of Abraham's life, he searched for the city and, when he had finally found it, it was a great blessing for him to die. In fact, it was a great blessing for all of God's people in the Old Testament time to die, and Hebrews 11:33-39 explains why.

> Who through faith subdued kingdoms, wrought righteousness, obtained promises, stopped the mouths of lions,
>
> Quenched the violence of fire, escaped the edge of the sword, out of weakness were made strong, waxed valiant in fight, turned to flight the armies of the aliens.
>
> Women received their dead raised to life again: and others were tortured, not accepting deliverance; that they might obtain a better resurrection:
>
> And others had trial of cruel mockings and scourgings, yea, moreover of bonds and imprisonment:
>
> They were stoned, they were sawn asunder, were tempted, were slain with the sword: they wandered about in sheepskins and goatskins; being destitute, afflicted, tormented;
>
> (Of whom the world was not worthy:) they wandered in deserts, and in mountains, and in dens and caves of the earth.
>
> And these all, having obtained a good report through faith, received not the promise.

Regardless of persecution suffered, the Bible says that they had great victory and received many of the promises. In the Old Testament, people gladly suffered affliction and were gladly put to death, as the Word says in the latter part of verse 35.

Those who loved God in the Old Testament days looked forward to dying, and somehow that attitude has spilled over into 20th century Christianity. Many Christians think the reason that they suffer persecution and affliction is so that "someday" they can be free.

But the truth is that the Old Testament saints looked forward to dying because they were living under the Old Covenant and the fulfillment of the promise of a better life was found in dying.

Yet, even under the Old Covenant, they did all that is listed in the above verses and some Christians can't even get rid of a cold under the New Covenant! The New Covenant was implemented and fulfilled in the man Christ Jesus. We have a better covenant today than Abraham ever dreamed of as verse 40 says: **God having provided some better thing for us.**

What better thing has God provided for us? Hebrews 5:9 answers this in reference to Jesus:

And being made perfect, he became the author of eternal salvation unto all them that obey him.

An author is one who writes; therefore, we must pay attention to His words. A study of the words *salvation, perfect,* and *eternal* in Greek provides further depth into the truth contained in the above verse:

Salvation: to be rescued or ransomed from all bondage and sickness or death. Salvation means that we were rescued from these things, never having to receive them again. We aren't looking for that city because *we are already there.* We are not Abraham or Job but a born-again individual living the New Covenant life. Hebrews 8:13 says, **In that he saith, A new covenant, he hath made the first old.**

In other words, God has replaced the Old Covenant with a new, better, and eternal covenant. We must get the promises, available through this New Covenant, into our spirits so that we can claim what is rightfully ours. We could have had all the rich promises that Abraham had, yet God looked down and gave us better ones by sending His Son to suffer and die on Calvary to ratify a New Covenant between God and man.

Jesus signed that covenant with the ink of His blood and wrote it across the canvas of eternity for all ages.

The next word, *perfect,* is described as meaning *complete* or *finished.* Many people think that we receive the fulfillment of this promise only when we die. However, spiritual, not physical, death is the key to this particular fulfillment. Spiritual death causes us to enter into the New Covenant believership which, in turn, allows us to enter into the fulfillment of promises.

> **Who his own self bare our sins in his own body on the tree, that we, being dead to sins, should live unto righteousness: by whose stripes ye were healed.**
>
> **1 Peter 2:24**

When Jesus went to Calvary, he did it for you and me, because He already had defeated the devil. The Man without a spot or blemish took every ugly sin upon His shoulders and bore our sicknesses, our diseases, and our loneliness as well.

We cry about how lonely we are, yet Jesus was the only person to really know what loneliness was. We do not know what it was like to be on that Golgotha hillside, somewhere between Heaven and earth, with the sun beating on our brows and flies roaming in and out of our open wounds and gnawing on our flesh. God, Himself, had to turn His own eyes away from His only Son saying, in essence, "I can't even look at Him." The world rejected Him, even those who loved Him, yet Jesus bore loneliness that we might be free from it.

Jesus was intent on going to Calvary so that He could put to death the vile sins, the sicknesses, and the infirmities of the world. As they took His hand and held it open, nailing it deep into the wooden cross, sickness died. When they drove the other hand into the other side of the cross, sin died. When they nailed His feet down, loneliness died.

He looked up to the Father, and cried out, **My God, My God, why hast Thou forsaken me?** Then He spoke again: **Father, into thy hands I commend my Spirit,** bowed His head and said, **It is finished.** (Mark 15:34; Luke 23:46; John 19:30.)

The Old Covenant had just passed away and glorious light had risen over the horizon. Sin and death ruled no longer as they had been nullified by the law of life in Christ Jesus! The blood sings out over the bygone millenniums of time; and, *we are free at last!* Any time the devil tries to come against you, serve notice on him by saying, "I don't live under the Old Covenant, for I have been ransomed by the blood of Jesus that cleanses me from all unrighteousness and heals all of my diseases."

Years ago, when communications were much slower than now, thousands of men and women were killed in war, after a peace treaty was signed, simply because the combatants hadn't received word that the war was over. When Jesus said it was over, the peace treaty was signed, the healing treaty was signed, and the prosperity treaty was signed. The devil was defeated and still is, because the war is over and Jesus won! However, some Christians, apparently, have yet to hear the news.

The last word, *eternal*, is described as existing at all times, past, present, and future. This word denotes no beginning and no ending. God is eternal. He always has been and always will be. He is an eternal being;

a Spirit with no beginning and no ending. In John, chapter 3, Jesus explained how a person can receive the eternal life of God:

> There was a man of the Pharisees, named Nicodemus, a ruler of the Jews:
>
> The same came to Jesus by night, and said unto him, Rabbi, we know that thou art a teacher come from God: for no man can do these miracles that thou doest, except God be with him.
>
> Jesus answered and said unto him, Verily, verily, I say unto thee, Except a man be born again, he cannot see the kingdom of God.
>
> Nicodemus saith unto Him, How can a man be born when he is old? Can he enter the second time into his mother's womb, and be born?
>
> Jesus answered, Verily, verily, I say unto thee, Except a man be born of water and of the Spirit, he cannot enter into the kingdom of God.
>
> That which is born of the flesh is flesh; and that which is born of the Spirit is spirit.
>
> Marvel not that I said unto thee, Ye must be born again.
>
> The wind bloweth where it listeth, and thou hearest the sound thereof, but canst not tell whence it cometh, and whither it goeth: so is everyone that is born of the Spirit.
>
> John 3:1-8

We are born of the Spirit of God, which means our mortal bodies came in contact with something that has no beginning and no ending. Eternal life is an existence that will continue forever! When you became born again, the flow of eternal life just picked up your mortal body as an agent and began to flow through you.

How do I know that God created the earth, that Jesus wiped the blindness from Bartimaeus' eyes, and that He rose again from the dead? Because I was there when it happened. I can say that because I have received the Spirit of God that has always existed and shall always exist. When we are born again, we come in contact with an eternal, living God Who transfers His Spirit, which has no beginning and no ending, into us.

Abraham looked for the city that represented the kingdom of God. But where is the kingdom? The answer is found in Luke.

> And when he was demanded of the Pharisees, when the kingdom of God should come, he answered them and said, The kingdom of God cometh not with observation:
>
> Neither shall they say, Lo here! or, lo there! for, behold, the kingdom of God is within you.
>
> Luke 17:20,21

The city that Abraham looked for with all of its blessings and promises is now resident in your body. **The kingdom of Heaven is within you,** meaning that you rule and reign and are an overcomer and a conqueror in this life because you no longer live under the Old Covenant but are established in the New. Let's quit looking for tomorrow and start living for today!

I encourage you to step into the light of the *present-day truth* which is the only doorway leading out of the "Someday Syndrome."

> This book of the law shall not depart out of thy mouth; but thou shalt meditate therein day and night, that thou mayest observe to do according to all that is written therein: for then thou shalt make thy way prosperous, and then thou shalt have good success.
>
> Joshua 1:8

> And he began to say unto them, This day is this scripture fulfilled in your ears.
>
> Luke 4:21

37

BOOKS AND CASSETTE TAPES

by Rodney L Parsley

Cassette Tapes

The Day of the Lord Cometh
Righteousness
Stir Up the Gift
A Reflection of Glory
Set in the Church
The Church: A Reservoir or A River
Antidote to Current Demonic Influence

All of the above are available at:

**Word of Life Ministries
10165 Wright Rd
Canal Winchester, OH 43110**

Books

The Laws of Sowing and Reaping
I See an Underground Church
Tradition, The Thief of Power
Worshipping the Unknown God

*Books available both at the above address and at your
local Christian bookstore or directly from:*

**Albury Press
P.O. Box 55388
Tulsa, OK 74155**